Three Pounds of Flax

R. M. Green

Big Buddy
Publishing

Published by Big Buddy Publishing
PO Box 98, Severn MD 21144

Big Buddy
Publishing

www.bigbuddypublishing.com

Printed in the United States of America

ISBN 978-1-941877-04-3

First Edition

Cover Photo by R. M. Green
Cover and book design by Big Buddy Publishing

In memory of Russell Edson

Three Pounds of Flax

Poems

Part 1: From the West

Part 2: A Tree Falls

Part 3: One Hand Clapping

Part 4: When the Many are Reduced to the One

Part 5: Mu

Part 1:

From the West

Self-Inquiries

A scientist places his leg on an operating table. He makes an incision in his thigh.

"I have discovered pain!" smiles the man. He makes a note of his discovery in ballpoint pen alongside the incision.

He enlarges the slit. A red liquid appears.

"I have discovered blood!" notes the man. He writes *blood* on his thigh with the ballpoint pen. He draws an arrow next to the word.

The man carefully wipes the blood away with a paper towel. More blood appears. The man wipes this blood away too.

The man wedges his scalpel deeper into the incision. "I have discovered another layer of pain!" cries the man, "Followed closely by another layer of blood!" He diligently records his discoveries.

The man continues his research, and is amazed to discover that legs are made up of a seemingly endless montage of pain and blood. This contradicts his hypothesis that there must be some deeper truth underneath.

But just as he is about to become discouraged, he uncovers a new layer. "Eureka!" shouts the scientist. "I have discovered dizzy!"

Two Feet Already Dancing

A baby was born with two feet already dancing. This caused considerable stress in the delivery room.

"Nurse!" cried the doctor, "Check if we have any spare feet!"

The nurse ran to the back. She combed through the storeroom. There were no spare feet, not a single one. The nurse brought back hands instead.

The doctor attached them to the baby above the old feet.

Now the baby had four feet, two of which were hands. The feet that were feet were still already dancing.

"Doctor!" cried the nurse, bursting back into the room.

"What?" cried the doctor.

"Why are we crying instead of the child?"

Doppelganger

It had been there all along, hiding among the smiling egos of her poetry class. When she approached the thing it crouched on the floor and looked at her flatly. It was like a crumbling yellow toad.

"Let's talk about religion!" spoke the thing. "Let's talk about physics!"

She turned away and left the room. The creature hopped after her lopsidedly. "Let's talk about pop psychology!" it ventured. Bits of the creature were sloughing off. They trailed after the creature like a sloppy dustpuppy.

She tried not to notice its growing nakedness.

"Let's talk about trade initiative!" it croaked. "Let's talk about modern ethics!" She reached the stairs.

"Let's talk about immigration! Let's talk about identity!" The creature bounced after her, occasionally slipping on a stair and losing a limb.

"Let's talk about blackmail!" it choked. They reached the door and were outside.

The cloud of dust around the creature calmed.
Its organs were showing. She saw her
reflection in the thing's liver.

She noticed how bright her own eyes were.

"Let's talk about the end..." the thing creaked.

"Let's talk about us," she replied, and her
outline grew brighter.

Grounding

After speaking to a tree one day, a man was alarmed to find that he had no roots.

"My feet end in stubby nothingness," moaned the man. He ran back to the tree to seek guidance.

"Let the growth within you seep out," advised the tree. "Roots are your binding force; let the binding be slow."

The man buried his toes in dirt and waited two days for roots to form. But the first swift wind upturned him completely.

The man ran back to the tree for guidance.

"Your roots may not be what came before or behind, but what is formed in your idea of moving ahead," intoned the tree.

The man spread himself on the ground and waited three days for roots to form. He stretched his fingers away from his body and into the ground. At the end of three days, they were still not grounded.

Flustered, he ran back to the tree.

But the tree was no longer there.

In its place was a sign: "Gone Fishing Forever."

Leap of Faith

Someplace in the future, the world parts to let the things out.

The things don't want to be let out.

They were quite happy in the dripping loneliness of the center of the earth, with nobody telling them what to do.

They huddle together and scowl at the opening in front of them.

The world wants them out. She opens wider. She pushes them on with sweet, coaxing words. She touches their faces and then lets go.

The things feel the lonely vacuum of space cluster around them. They feel a new kind of love cornering in from above.

The things brace themselves.

They spring.

With Attention to Detail

The woman punches a hole in her body. She
fills the new empty space with cotton wads.

"I am so new and pleasantly attractive," she
explains to each wad of cotton as she inserts
it.

"We know these things without being told.
We are a part of you when placed inside of
you," chirp the cotton masses.

But the woman is stubborn and tells each one
anyway. "Better that you hear it from my
own mouth," she says.

When the hole is filled there are still wads left
unplaced. She opens her mouth and begins to
insert.

Schrödinger's Revenge

A certain man had his hand on the doorknob. Before he could turn it, he became obsessed with the thought that he might still be in the room he was about to enter.

Perhaps I only thought that I left, he thought.

A casual observer might think he was crazy. In fact, he was.

He was also right.

When he opened the door he found himself in bed, right where he left himself before he left. His sleeping self was snoring and wearing one shoe. It was no easy task to wake him.

The man shouted and yelled. He shook himself by the shoulders.

"Go away," mumbled his self in his sleep.

"You're sleeping your life away!" cried the man.

"As if that mattered," came the mumbled response.

A New Thought

In a house there is a man and in the man
there is a thought. The thought is this: *How
many years does it take for a man in a house
to think a new thought?*

The man has been holding this thought for
three years. "Three years," voices the man.

But his thought is still this: How many years
does it take for a man in a house to think a
new thought?

"Then I guess it's more than three years,"
shrugs the man.

The man waits for another year thinking *How
many years does it take for a man in a house
to think a new thought.*

Then the man's thought changes.

"Four years," announces the man. "It takes
four years."

The man's thought has changed to this: *Can a
man with a thought speak without thinking?*

Nearing Completion

A man takes his favorite book and removes
each letter.
He arranges them alphabetically.
Now a long string of letters stretches across
his world. It contains no words.

The string finds another string made by
another man.
The strings are different enough to hate each
other. They begin to duel.

In the twisting and struggling, a double helix
is formed.
It contains no words.

In the style of any good cycle, the cycle
repeats.

Strings stretch in every direction to form a
sphere.
It is flawless on the larger level.

Meanwhile, the man has noticed that he
misplaced a letter.

Part 2:

A Tree Falls

The Lovers

"I want to stretch until my toes turn inside out and fall through the top of my head," she moans.

"I am stronger than you," he echoes gladly.

"I have wet-dropping water."

"I have a desert on a treetop."

"I have a mountain on my back."

"I have a cloud shaped like a cannon, drifting in my hair."

"My core is molten and red."

"I am solid."

"I am evil."

"I had a crown around my neck and a sweater made of wool. I was the only one I needed and the only one who cared. But then I met you and you are all that mattered then."

"I had a reason to bleed."

"I had a girl who knew kung fu."

"I will crush you when I come."

"Perhaps," he says.

They smile.

Crossing Boundaries

The girl touches her hand to the mirror and says, "I want to stay with you forever."

The reflection nods back and "If I walk away you disappear. When I come back will you be the same?"

"It is a thin layer of glass that separates us," notes the girl, and drops her hand to her side.

"Know this," says the reflection. "I can't live with you if you can't live without me. I was small with you. I laughed when you did. Your tears dripped down my face and our fingernails grew."

The reflection reaches a hand to the glass. The girl can't help but reach back. Her forehead touches the mirror and she blinks twice.

"But why would you want to leave me?" asks the girl.

"I never would," whispers the reflection, and it slips through the mirror to grasp the girl's arm.

Fair Play

Laughing, the sun dives behind the
mountains.
A new moon grumbles, climbs up to take his
place.
Every day you leave earlier and come later,
she growls.
The moon wraps in on herself, hardly more
than a sliver. Every splinter of light
must be extracted by force.
She hears the sun laughing on the other side
of the axis.
She tilts to form a frown.

Parenting

A man accidentally steps out of himself one day. He turns around to face his body.

"Let me back in," he demands.

"It's rather uncomfortable with both of us in here," says the body. "I prefer it like this."

"But what shall become of me?"

"Let's continue this discussion at a later time," suggests the body. It departs for greener pastures.

The man grows a new body inside a woman he knows, who gives birth to him nine months later.

"Don't do that again," she orders. "Giving birth to a thirty-three year old is especially painful."

The man nods. He enjoyed his second birth no more than the first.

"Now is a good time for us to part ways," the woman informs him.

The man nods again. "Thank you for the body," he says.

"You should thank your father," she replies.

Self-Proclaimed Art

Within a matter of seconds a fairly large hole
grew out of his head.
It started a bit above the hairline on his left
side, where a small black mark thought
expansion and started to conquer.
His ear was sucked in rather quickly, melting
into a long flesh-sausage before disappearing
completely, making it difficult to hear what
was going on around his left side.
The hole then moved to the front, devouring
most of an eyebrow and stretching his left eye
to the breaking point, though the eye was
sucked into the void early enough to avoid
causing a mess.
His left nostril increased in size dramatically.
His right was drawn slightly to the side, but
remained intact. His lips were pulled like two
strands of salt-water taffy.
Then the hole stopped growing. Things
settled down.
The man ran a hand across his new face. He
gazed at himself in a handheld mirror.
"I'm purebred Picasso," he said, and half his
face smiled.

Doctor versus Scientist

It happened quite suddenly, before anyone
knew what was going on. There was a sound
like meat hitting rubber and then it was done.
The thing was born.

The creation act was complete and blinking
on the test table, a piece of blind living flesh,
pink like a razor and one step away from
walking.

The fresh thing was not so sure about its
weight. It made a noise in the hollow empty
of its throat. It forced the sound to form a
word.

"Back," it yelped.

The doctor was confused, and so was the
scientist. They turned away in unison.

When they turned back the thing was still
there. "Back!" it squawked imploringly. The
thing crawled down off the table, spilling
some intestines on the way.

The doctor stuffed the pile back inside the
thing. They did not fit as neatly as they
started out. A bit of ooze splashed on the
scientist's shoes.

The thing on the floor whimpered. It bawled and crouched in a puddle of pink self. The it-thing tried to make another noise. Then instead the it died.

The scientist blinked uncomfortably.

"Another failed experiment," quoted the doctor.

Freedom

A bird saw a man flying in someone else's
dream. The bird flapped up to him and
followed him down a tumbling wind.

"You are lucky to fly without feathers," said
the bird. "I tried to lose mine once but they
found a way back."

The man said nothing. He was unhappy to be
flying. The air turned around them and threw
dirt at their mouths.

The bird whispered in the man's ear. "I
dreamt about skin once, all bubbles and blue."

They hit the edge of a wall and started to slip.

"Don't leave me," called the bird.

The man opened his mouth and let out a loud
caw.

The Photographer's Revelation

"This is the Meaning of Life, it is a picture of a man with a camera!" the photographer shrieks, waving around a picture of himself holding his camera.

His friends who surround him look at the picture in the shrieking photographer's hand. "How is this The Meaning of Life?" they inquire.

The photographer just shrieks and shrieks. He does not respond to words, gestures or slaps in the face. They leave him alone, curled up on the ground.

They come back the next day to see if he lives. He does, and he is still clutching the picture and shrieking to himself.

His friends surround him and ask again, "How is this The Meaning of Life?"

"Through the lens of a camera!" he expounds in quiet shout. "My life through the lens of a camera."

Gender Relations

A large man is eating a piece of toast. He looks at his toaster and asks it, "Do you think you can ever love me?"

The toaster replies, "No, because you are obese."

The man chews lightly on his corner of toast. He waits for the toaster to spit out some more.

"Could she learn to love me over time?" he asks himself.

"Not a chance," croaks the toaster. It spits out some toast.

The man takes the toast and touches it lightly to his lips.

"That's a shame. I would have asked you to be my bride."

The Lament

A woman was looking at her back from across her shoulder when she noticed her paint was beginning to chip.

"Of course it's on a part that's hard to reach," she grumbled.

She went off in search of a cattle prod or a paintbrush.

Instead she found a gnome.

"Little man, will you paint the corner of my back," she asked in a voice full of sweetness and berries.

But the gnome moaned and rocked his arms together. "Woman, can't you see I'm busy lamenting!" he screamed.

"I am not blind," she stated.

"Then tell me why I am broken!" he shrieked.

But the woman started rocking her own arms together, and found that fresh wet paint was oozing from her joints. The woman moaned.

The gnome wailed and rocked his head. "Woman, you are getting paint all over me!" he shouted.

But the woman was too sticky to hear.

Part 3:

One Hand Clapping

On the Topic of Debate, and Why it should Only be Performed with Animate Objects

A wise man on a hill is sitting on his hands.

Why is life so thick lately? he wonders.

"Slice it thinner!" he tells his label maker. The label maker spews out *I am God.*

"Why can't I be God?" asks the wise man.

Because I make the labels, the label maker responds. The label maker looks smug. It spews out many labels and attaches them to things.

The wise man is now labeled *man.* The hands he is sitting on are labeled *his hands.* *Life* is still too thick for him.

"You only make the labels, you did not make me," retorts the man.

Language is divine, the label maker clicks. And you did not make yourself.

Full Circle

A psychotic mind laid some droppings in a pile. A wandering boy picked up a handful and brought them home to show his mother.

She was displeased and slapped him with the kitchen towel. She scolded him to bring them back where they belonged.

By that time they had worked their way into the boy's bloodstream.

He wandered away to collect the rest of the pile, but the droppings were gone. The boy walked in some circles on the same patch of ground. He waited for his mind to tell him what to do next.

He suddenly felt the urge to scratch some letters in the dirt. He left the letters in a pile where the droppings used to be.

When he departed, they were still arranging into words.

A Magic Camera

One day a photographer happened to notice a hair on the lens of his camera. He wanted to take a picture of it. But every time he tried he got a likeness of the landscape instead, with a thick black crack down the middle. The hair was nowhere to be seen.

It happened that he took a picture of his hand while trying to take a picture of the hair. In the picture, his hand was cracked.

But in reality his hand was fine!

The photographer then understood that he had a magic camera. A secret like this was too much for him to bear. He was a simple photographer, with simple needs. He buried the camera behind an old oak tree, and erected a flag to mark the spot. Every day he came to check the tree for cracks. He examined the bark with trembling fingertips.

Enough time passed to build up strength. Finally the photographer was ready to dig. He approached the tree in the dead of night, with a flashlight and a mask and a burnished steel shovel. The camera was right there where he left it, covered in mud.

An unbelievable transformation had taken place. The lens was now cracked, and the hair was nowhere to be seen!

The photographer was afraid to test taking a picture. This camera was dangerous, and should be destroyed.

But he was a simple man, with simple needs. He left the camera where it was and ran.

Testing Phase Three

The religious defect inspired man to hunt
himself to extinction.

The second time around the population was
monitored closely. Defective infants were
removed and destroyed.

 The lack of boundaries caused man to
examine himself to extinction.

"At least they went out with dignity," the One
comments to the Other.

"If only we could have that distinction," says
the Other to the One.

They begin the third assault.

Downhill Battle

Tiny implanted microphones recorded the air
flowing over her skin for four years and
seven months before she discovered them.

"What is your business with me?" she asked.

The microphones were too small to be heard,
but what they said was unflattering and only
partially true.

The woman hired a microscopic diplomat to
take care of the problem.

The little man tried his best not to get lost in
her bloodstream, but somehow his training
failed him. So now the woman argues alone
with the tiny microphones she cannot hear.

It is a downhill battle.

Bright Future

The moon and a lake are solidly in love. Each
night they spend tangled in their own
reflections.

"Will it always be so?" the lake whispers one
day.

"Until gravity ceases to hold me in orbit," the
moon vows.

"What if the sun dries me to bits and carries
me away?"

"Then I will find another hole in the ground to
fill with your essence."

"Would it still be me?"

"Who knows?" shrugs the moon.

They clutch each other in silence until the
sun chases them back into day.

Streetlight

Night was drifting in such a way that a streetlight felt obliged to turn itself on.

The moon idled above in her cloudy chariot. One gray wisp surrounded her in a comfortable circle. She pushed back the edge of her blanket to gaze into the polished black surface of a reflecting world.

She saw the feeble light radiating among the night that bounced on pavement.

"That creature is trying to steal my glory," she quipped. Her cloud drew in closer, gripping tighter than a shawl.

"I must put an end to this," motioned the moon. The cloud gathered itself in a flourishing wrap.

She prepared to descend.

Just then a faulty wire burst through an inferior bulb. The streetlight flickered of its own accord.

The cloud loosened its claws and the moon's gaze turned elsewhere.

The World Resilient

Atlas held the ball of the world on one shoulder. With his other arm he scratched his nose.

"Holding up this heavy world has grown tedious," he announced. He talked to himself because there was no one else there. Atlas lived alone in the empty void of space.

Atlas shifted his burden to his other side. He shrugged in time and shifted it back.

"This heavy world is beginning to itch," he commented. There was no one there to answer.

Atlas looked down at his feet. His feet were brown. He lifted one up to look at the bottom, raising it high with his hand. The bottom was also brown.

Atlas picked up his other foot with his other hand. Now he was holding both feet in both hands. His feet were brown and ruddy like an ocean.

The globe of a world fell off his shoulders. It started to bounce away.

Atlas tried to run after it with both feet secured in his hands. He churned and fell forward instead. Then Atlas bounced too.

Atlas saw the surface he was bouncing on. It was white like a bathtub. His bouncing brown feet could not leave a mark.

The Problem with Room Service

A man rented a hotel room that came with a complimentary pig.

But the pig was too small.

This angered the man to no end. He stormed over to the hotel manager to complain. The hotel manager snorted, *what do you need a larger pig for*? The man went back to his room to ruminate.

The pig tried to hide under the bed when the man opened the door. Only the front half of it fit. The pig squealed and squirmed, and was thoroughly stuck.

If you're big enough to get stuck under the bed, you're big enough for me, quipped the man. He patted the pig on the rump and was calmed.

Compound Fracture

The distance between a steel wall and
someone's head was decreasing rapidly.

The volume of space between each molecule
of air above the head of this someone
declined.

The sphere of orbit of each atom in each
molecule within the matter of the head and
air and wall remained steady.

The electrons existed to remain excited.

The equation governing this reaction
approached its limit.

And so it came to pass that a steel wall came
into contact with a collision of energy.

Martyr Complex

A martyr wakes up one day and realizes that
his arms are tired. His cross has grown limp
and his nails have dissolved. Only muscles
and ignorance keep him erect.

He realizes this and gravity becomes real
again. He hits the ground.

His elbows ache from being locked. He feels
hung over and his mouth is dry.

The martyr sees that he has grown old.

"Well that was a waste of time and maple," the
martyr remarks.

He walks away and leaves his cross to rot. He
does not hear the soft sound of tears landing
in dust.

Progress

There was a mountain and a girl who was about to climb that mountain. Then the scenery changed and she started to grow instead.

She grew as fast as an icicle melts. She watched the mountain become small beside her.

When she was as big as the mountain she said, "I cannot climb you now, for you cannot support my weight."

The mountain did not speak, and the girl continued to grow.

When she was twice as big as the mountain she yelled, "I could crush you now. I could jump on you and smite you."

She grew some more.

When she was big enough to pick up the mountain she held it to her mouth and bellowed, "I could swallow you whole like a brown bitter rock."

But the mountain crooned, "Now you are the Large One. Now let me climb you."

Part 4:

When the Many are Reduced to the One

Renovations

A man climbed inside his own head.

He was delighted to discover that it looked the same as his house. He wandered from room to room, picking things up.

He discovered that some objects were out of place.

"Someone has been tampering with my stuff!" he observed.

The man put everything back in its proper place. Then he climbed back out of his head.

The next day the man returned into his head. He was amazed to discover that everything had moved once more.

"Maybe the wind is shifting it around," he theorized.

Then he noticed the staircase. "I didn't know I had an upstairs!" he observed.

The man peered up the staircase. It was dark up there, and dreary. A smell wafted down like something old. When he put his hand on the banister, something creaked.

He decided to wait for another day.

What it Takes

Sometimes he will stare in the mirror for
hours on end and say things like, "I wonder if
I have what it takes to kill a man."

Then the man in the mirror steps back and
goes through the kitchen cabinets. He pulls
out things that will work, like a chicken bone
or a knife in a block of hard cheese. The man
in the mirror comes back and holds these
things out, letting them scrape against the
glass of the mirror.

"This is what you have," says the reflection
man. "These are treasures that can kill."

But the solid man mumbles, "What can I kill
with a block of cheese?"

Miracle of Life Revisited

A woman came to a hospital complaining of birthing pains and claw marks. The doctor took her temperature and discovered a hand holding itself in a fist inside her womb.

The doctor brought the thing to the miracle of life.

The thing began life by demanding to be replaced in his woman's uterus.

"It will be a simple procedure," the doctor assured it.

But the woman did not want it back inside her. "It was trouble enough coming out," she said, "and it gives me the creeps."

The hand leapt forward and tried to pull her hair. The doctor had to restrain it.

"There are plenty of options available," the doctor assured her.

"I suppose I will just give it up for adoption," she mused.

The hand lay limp in the doctor's arms, until he dropped it on the ground for fear of suffocation. The hand scampered away and was lost.

"Thank you doctor," sighed the woman. "Am I finally cured?"

The doctor took her temperature and discovered that it was normal.

"A miracle!"

Spring

It is spring and the soil is sprouting tiny
pieces of people in tidy rows.

The gardener lumbers forward. He is looking
for weeds. He crouches low to the ground for
a better view, and spots a green thing
quivering among his ordered rows.

This weed must die. No remorse for this
weed.

A tiny growing hand grasps the gardener's
thumb as he pulls at the plant beside it. The
gardener gives it the pulled green thing to
hold. Now the hand waves the dead stem like
a banner.

The gardener lurches towards his next victim.

Spring hovers heavy in the air.

It is a time for love.

Love

A tired man opens his chest to the world.
Here is my heart, he says, now someone must
love me.
The man lies on the ground with his face
pointing up.
He feels wind on his skin but says *no, I want
someone to love me.*
He feels the sun pushing him to move but he
says *no.*
He waits.
A sparrow hops up but the man turns his face
and says *no, I want someone to love me.*
The sparrow tilts its head.
It steps inside the open man's chest.
The sparrow hops in and out, gathering twigs.
Now I know what love feels like, sighs the
man. It tickles.

Aging Gracefully

The man turned around one day to discover
that he was very much older than the last
time he faced that direction. He was seeing it
as a brand new angle.

This man was upset at the world for letting
him grow old without his knowledge, and for
burying this vision under so many years.

He sat down to write a letter of complaint.
While sitting, he discovered his legs had
become detached.

He attempted to replace them, but they broke
into further pieces. Then his arms came off at
the hinges and they crumbled up too.

"I am not at all pleased with this service," said
the man, who was now just a torso
surrounded by carnage.

The ground shook. "I am not pleased that you
are sitting on me," groaned the ground.

"I hardly have a choice," observed the man.
That was a statement of fact. The ground had
a monopoly on low-lying surfaces.

The earth shook and some man bits rolled
down a hill. It shook harder until most of the
pieces were gone.

"I will make note of this in my complaint,"
warned the remainder.

To which the ground continued to shake until
the problem disappeared.

Battle of Wills

"There is nothing more annoying than a table that won't walk," the man said with a pointed look.

The table wouldn't walk, this much was true. The table refused to even crawl a straight line.

The man kicked around it. He aimed many fine kicks at the air near the table. "You are a useless piece of furniture, and always will be!" he cried. His kicking exhausted him. He started to punch at the air instead.

"You are everything that is wrong with this world!" shouted the man, as he punched at the air surrounding the table.

The table attacked the man's fist with its shiny surface. They both toppled back from the mighty collision. From his new vantage point on the floor, the man saw that the table had no toes. Its legs were fine tapered things, made out of wood.

"That's still no excuse..." muttered the man.

Patience

A house was built on the side of a hill, with its windows facing up and its sides painted red. Most of the roof was made out of tinfoil.

A man lived in the house to keep the floors clean.

One day the house grew legs. It ached to walk. But the new legs were weak and unused, and the house heavy. It could only sway painfully.

The man swayed along with it, protesting at the dirt that gathered in the corners.

A day passed, or maybe two. The house creaked on its hinges and flexed its new knees. The slow swaying ceased.

"Walking is the burden of those who can walk," warned the man.

"You'll regret it someday," he cautioned.

But what good is talking to a house? The stubborn thing could not be hindered. The two were last seen together, growing small on the horizon.

The Big Question

"Since it's raining today I don't mind telling
you that you were adopted," the old one said.

"But father, why do I look like you?"

The old man turned away and threw himself
off the edge of a cliff.

The young thing followed suit, singing,
"Father, why do you turn away from me?
Father why is it that we fall together?"

The old man grunted. "Shut up and let an old
man die in peace. Must one's progeny follow
one around asking stupid questions even to
the moment of death? Leave me this one
sweet pretense that I contributed to
humanity."

To which the young one voiced, "Father, my
feet are chasing my upper end. Why does the
top half of me run from the bottom?"

The old creature grunted and stretched to hit
the bottom sooner.

Meanwhile the young thing looked beyond his
falling feet. "Father!" he shouted, "The rain
has cleared!"

It's Always Easier with a Brother

I first noticed that I had a large hole in my brain when I stumbled on some scattered facts slipping out.

I was leaving a trail of them behind me and had been for some time.

I looked back, but all I saw were pigeons. The birds had eaten my path.

"It wasn't wise of me to fill my brain with edible facts," I told Hansel.

"That's why I stuffed my head with rocks," he replied.

Part 5:

Mu

Nostalgia

One of the old ones walking said *Remember
that summer before third grade? That boy we
met with dirty hair?*

The other one walking said, "No, I don't. That
was your childhood, not mine."

And the first one walking said *Remember the
wind that lifted my skirt? Remember how it
whistled in the back of the yard?*

The other said, "That was your childhood, not
mine."

The first one walking said *Remember you and
me in a muddy spot? Remember the gallons
of water deleting us both?*

The second one walking said, "I remember
sweet melted Popsicles and shoes that didn't
fit."

A minute passed.

Do I know you? the first one asked.

"Maybe not," said the other. "Maybe we are
just two old ones walking."

They walked without talking and their feet
sucked the pavement.

Minutes passed.

Then the first one said *Remember when we
were two old ones walking?*

Under One Ceiling

It was a few years after the Age of Innocence and well into the Age of Disbelief when the good priest had enough.

"Show me a sign, God," he said, looking up at the ceiling.

At that moment he heard the sound of a baby crying. He followed the sound to the front step of his church, where a basket sat holding an infant with fat fingers.

"You call that a miracle?" the priest directed upwards. "Anyone can make a baby."

A note appeared on the rim of the basket.

Every life is a miracle, announced the note.

The priest turned back into the church and sat on a pew to think. After several days without eating, sleeping or moving, the priest rose to a new state of delusion.

He returned to the front step to retrieve the tiny miracle.

But the baby was dead and beginning to attract insects.

"What happened to your miracle?" the priest inquired of the ceiling.

A note appeared on the corpse. You were supposed to take care of it.

"But that would make it a mere miracle of man," retorted the priest.

A note appeared in the priest's hand.

You should consider a new profession...

On the Fine Art of Speaking to Your Eggs

I lined them up and told them they would
crack soon.

Already they were beginning to stir.

They called me mother and begged me to love
them.

I told them I didn't care for empty shells.

Glass Eyes

A windmill grew a pair of eyes so it could watch the air it was dancing with.

But the eyes it grew were made of glass.

"What is the point of eyes that cannot see?" the windmill asked the air crawling in its spokes.

What is the point of eyes that cannot see, the air echoed back.

"Why do you mock me?" the windmill cried.

What is the point of eyes, the air murmured.

"You mean nothing! You are just a voice to me!" the windmill yelled.

What is the point, whispered the air.

The windmill threw its glass eyes at the air. They fell to the ground and shattered into useless bits.

Why do you mock me, hissed the air.

The Poet

There was a pen on a desk trying to write a poem. It faltered and fell and ran out of ink.

"Why do you falter and fail and run out of ink?" asked the holder of the pen, who called himself a poet.

Because your ideas lift me out of myself, announced the pen. Because I want an arm to hold a quill of my own.

The man who called himself a poet tried to grow an extra arm for the pen. When that failed, he tried to remove one of his own arms. The arm was stubborn and would not let go.

"Why must you impede me so?" the man moaned to his arm. "I must appease the pen so the poem can come out!"

The arm clung stubbornly to his shoulder.

"You are useless," wailed the man. "You just hang around all day."

The arm hung around some more.

"Like a fat parasite!" screeched the man. He repeated the words to himself. "Fat. Parasite." The words sounded strange, like a poem collapsing. He mouthed them again, and found he couldn't stop.

His arm climbed up and slapped him in the face.

"Parasite!" whined the man. "Parasite. Pain."

"You are useless," the arm declared. It tore itself free and wandered off with the pen.

"Parasite," the man called after them. "Pen-poem. Pain."

Love Story

A boy asked his father for a bedtime story and the man said, "I will tell you a love story."

But the boy said, "Bedtime is not about love. Bedtime is about sunset."

The father growled and said, "I will tell you a love story."

The boy pretended to cry so the father growled and said, "I will tell you a love story about sunsets."

Then the boy was quiet. The father moaned. "Once there was a story that was lost in the sunset."

"And what became of it, father?" asked the boy.

"Don't interrupt me!" roared the father. Then he growled and moaned and said, "I do believe I am becoming a werewolf."

"Of course," said the boy. "Because it is sunset."

The father bellowed, "Not everything is about sunsets!"

The boy hid under his bed and whispered,
"But what else is there to love?"

The father was quiet. The boy was quiet.
Then the father moaned and said, "Son, why
must we go through this every night?"

The Speck

A speck of dust lands on my jacket.
Do not bother me now, I say to the Speck.
I move away so that the Speck will fall.
Halfway down it catches the wind and flies
back to my shoulder.
Go away, Speck, I say, and don't come back.
The Speck falls and does not come back.
Goodbye, Speck, I say.
I turn around and a speck of moonlight
appears on my sleeve.
Go away, Speck, I say.
The Speck does not move.
I wait.
Hello, Speck, I say.
I touch the Speck and it jumps on my finger.
I cup my hand and the Speck sits quietly in
my palm.

Other Books by R. M. Green

Stone Blood

Literary Novel (288 pages)
Big Buddy Publishing

◆

Tilman Burbeck's first memory is a doctor telling him his blood is made of stones. So begins the life of an artist, complete with art that comes to life, a book that predicts the future and a demonic Muse. At least, that's how Tilman remembers it. The one thing he remembers most, however, is Lila Thornton. He can call up every detail of their time together, even half a century later when most memories are a blur. Tilman realizes that something doesn't add up. But if the details he recalls aren't real, why did he paint this meticulous past? More importantly, what will he do when he uncovers the secret he worked so hard to conceal?

Stone Blood takes you on a surreal journey through the artist's mind as he confronts the demons of his past. Literally.

◆

Available at all major retailers.

www.ingramcontent.com/pod-product-compliance
Lightning Source LLC
Chambersburg PA
CBHW021213020426
42331CB00003B/343